the new york times

great songs of broadway

introductions by

alan jay lerner

and

jule styne

Quadrangle/The New York Times Book Co.

*With appreciation to **zinaida alexi** for believing*
in this book from beginning to end

First printing, March 1973

Library of Congress Catalog Card Number: 72-85051
International Standard Book Number: 8129-0288-2

Photo Credits
P. 11, Friedman-Abeles (George M)
P. 200, Friedman-Abeles (My Fair Lady/The Sound Of Music)
All other photos courtesy of Chappell & Co., Inc.

Music Typography: **Irwin Rabinowitz and Saul Honigman**
Music Proofreading: **Donald J. Jennings**
Jacket Design: **James S. Ward, Inc.**

Book Design: **Lee Snider**

Contents

Alan Jay Lerner: Introduction

Between the covers of this book are samples of the American musical theatre from the promising dawn of this century to the murky present. It is by no means a history of American popular music, although most of the songs contained herein not only became popular but achieved that special classification known in our profession as "standards." "Pop" music is one thing, theatre music is something else. In quality and execution, pop music can run the gamut from the gibberish of "Mairsey Doats" to the musicianship of "Stardust", from the ersatz folk and country music to the genuinely moving and expert "By The Time I Get To Phoenix." In the theatre, however, the dramatic demands placed on the score, the age and intelligence level of the theatre audience, plus the fangs of the critical watchdogs all combine to prevent the witless, the tasteless and the amateur from ever reaching the pages of a book such as this. All the composers and lyricists who authored these songs are (or were) serious writers and trained musicians, dedicated to their craft—professionals. (It is rather sad to note that the recent rebellion against literate professionalism has, for the most part, only produced illiterate commercialism.) The best example I can give of the difference between the depth of creation reached by a trained composer and a tune-writer is this: an untrained musician can pick out a tune with one finger on a piano that may very well become a hit, but—and I repeat—but, it will never—and I repeat—never, endure. A genuine composer may pick out a melody with one finger on the piano and it can last forever. As a simplistic but reasonably accurate generality one might say that theatre music is the highest form of popular music.

The American musical theatre actually began when the American legitimate theatre began: near the end of World War I. Up until then, our musical theatre was old Vienna, only in English, and the operettas of Stoltz, Kalman, Lehar and other ¾ time specialists were the national musical staple. The major exception was that incredible Jack-of-all-theatre-trades, George M. Cohan, who, at the turn of the century, was creating musicals with colloquial books and lyrics and a kind of educated Gay '90's music. Two of Cohan's perennial favorites begin the book, "Give My Regards To Broadway" and "I'm A Yankee Doodle Dandy." Both are marvelous songs. But the big explosion in theatre music started with Jerome Kern and the little musicals that he, P. G. Wodehouse and Guy Bolton wrote for the Princess Theatre in New York after World War I. These shows began what Oscar Levant was later to call the "classic period of American popular music."

Although operettas by such men as Friml and Romberg continued to flourish in the Twenties, now running right along side them was the new musical, the musical comedy, created by Kern, the Gershwins, Rodgers and Hart, Irving Berlin, DeSylva, Brown and Henderson, Dietz and Schwartz, Vernon Duke, Noel Coward, Cole Porter and others. The body of the work they created became the foundation of all theatre music and each is very properly represented in this collection.

When the stock market crashed in 1929 with a thud heard around the world, operetta's days were over. The disillusionment of the Depression could no more stand the rose-colored glasses of operetta than they could Herbert Hoover. As the institutions of the republic came under attack, the legitimate theatre became, to a large degree, a theatre of protest and musicals became brash and satiric; e.g., I'D RATHER BE RIGHT and PAL JOEY. The one exception was PORGY AND BESS, undoubtedly the all time towering achievement of the American musical theatre and George Gershwin's last show. Called an opera, it contained many dialogue passages and is by definition an opera comique. But the size of the music was operatic, operatic in a new and different way. We are not an aria country. We are a song country. And Gershwin stayed within the song idiom—expanded it, deepened it, heightened it to full aria dimension. "Summertime" is an example.

As the Depression had replaced the sentimental musical with satire, the war killed satire and revived the sentimental musical. The mood of the country switched like a traffic light to escape nostalgia and fantasy. The period that began with Rodgers and Hammerstein's OKLAHOMA in 1943 was in a sense the belle epoque of the musical theatre. For the first time text, music, lyrics and dance fused together in one pure dramatic entity and "the tired businessman's delight" suddenly became the lyric theatre. From the OKLAHOMA score, "Oh What A Beautiful Morning" and "The Surry With The Fringe On Top" are included in this volume. Other musicals of the time and genre also represented are CAROUSEL, FINIAN'S RAINBOW and BRIGADOON.

Not all composers and lyricists involved themselves in the changing styles of the musical theatre. One who did not was Cole Porter and frankly, who cared? Porter was so jubiliantly, romantically, brilliantly and uniquely Porter in every bar and every word that he wrote that the last thing one wanted to hear from him was a concession to the dramatic language of a character or anyone else. Unfortunately, it created problems for Porter himself because critically his work was constantly being under-valued. He told me that after he was initially hailed in the late Twenties, most of the time thereafter the usual review he received was that the score of the show that opened last night was not as good as his last one. Back in the thirties he was literally panned for JUBILEE and all that impoverished effort contained was "Begin The Beguine" and "Just One Of Those Things". The reviews for KISS ME, KATE were an exception. The score was simply too brilliant to be ignored. "Wunderbar" was one of its delicious moments.

By the late Forties the great burst of nostalgia and Americana provoked by the war ended. All the "fellers" and "purty gals" put away their sleeve garters and bloomers and lyrics began adding "g's" to words again. Musical books, however, had grown a bit and some kind of dramatic literacy and credibility continued to be expected of them. But authors began to feel humorous again and audiences began to feel more like laughing. But the laughter came more from characters than comics, more from situation than gags. When Bernard Shaw was a drama critic, he once wrote that he did not wish to be tickled to laughter, he wanted to be moved to laughter. Such was the trend of the musical book.

Musically, the overtones of operetta of the war years faded—but not completely. Anytime a baritone and soprano say something sincerely in music it will always seem musically a bit like operetta. The difference lies in what it is they are saying and how precisely and sensitively the composer dramatizes that particular emotion in terms of that particular character. On the surface, "Hello, Young Lovers," from THE KING AND I, is a lovely ballad of the French waltz variety that Dick Rodgers almost invented. What makes it considerably more and removes it from operetta is the poignancy of the lyric and the remembered joy of the melody that together are that woman at that moment.

In the Fifties, Cole Porter continued being Cole Porter and in his next show, CAN-CAN, he was subjected to his usual pounding. An enduring standard from CAN CAN is also included: "I Love Paris." Once he knew what he was going to write, Cole always worked back from the climax, and certainly the climax of "I Love Paris", the startling octave jump from minor to major, is Cole at his marvelous best.

In 1954, Porter wrote SILK STOCKINGS, the major song of which was "All Of You." After a rocky time on the road, the show came in a hit. But it was the last show he ever wrote for Broadway. My God, how he is missed! Cole was "the diamond as big as the Ritz."

Rodgers and Hammerstein followed THE KING AND I with ME AND JULIET in 1953. It was a backstage story that enjoyed a modest success. The best known song was "No Other Love," a haunting melody that Rodgers had originally composed for the background score of VICTORY AT SEA. Five years later they were represented again with FLOWER DRUM SONG and then, in 1959, they wrote THE SOUND OF MUSIC and thereby contributed one of the most unusual episodes in modern theatre history. Never was there a musical so viciously damned by the critics and so applauded by audiences the world over. One of Rodgers and Hammerstein's longest running hits, the film version became the box office champion of all times and the cast album from the film the number one movie cast album of all times. As Louis B. Mayer used to be fond of saying: "It was one of those plays nobody liked but the audience." One of the best known songs from the score was the first act curtain song, "Climb Ev'ry Mountain."

As the Fifties saw the last work of Cole Porter, THE SOUND OF MUSIC was the last show written by Oscar Hammerstein, one of the most beloved, respected and gifted men who ever wrote for the musical theatre. An incurable romantic and an unflagging idealist, Oscar Hammerstein wrote "Climb Ev'ry Mountain" while he was fighting a hopeless, agonizing battle for his life.

A major achievement of the musical theatre in the Fifties was WEST SIDE STORY, brilliantly conceived, directed and choreographed by Jerome Robbins, and with a soaring score by Leonard Bernstein and a new lyricist named Stephen Sondheim. In all the justifiable praise that WEST SIDE STORY received, it always seemed to me that Arthur Laurents never got his quota of recognition for the book. Thornton Wilder once said that more plays fail because of a breach in style than any other reason. As crucial as style is to a play, no less is it to a musical. And Arthur Laurents' book, with its moving re-telling of the Romeo and Juliet tale, its narrative economy and lyric language, and the skillful way it blends with the broad strokes of balletic storytelling is a triumph of style and model of its genre. As a fellow tradesman, I was filled with the deepest admiration.

Included in this collection are songs from four musical plays I wrote with Frederick Loewe: BRIGADOON in 1947, PAINT YOUR WAGON in 1951, MY FAIR LADY in 1956 and CAMELOT in 1960. From the mid-sixties there is the title song for ON A CLEAR DAY YOU CAN SEE FOREVER, for which Burton Lane was the composer. Further comments will be published posthumously.

These introductory notes should properly end with FIDDLER ON THE ROOF in 1964 because, in a very real sense, FIDDLER was the last in the line of musical plays that began with OKLAHOMA. Of course, there was a sprinkling of good musicals from 1964 to 1970 which this book will recall and some of them produced some very good songs. Certainly the song "Hello, Dolly!" is one of the great blockbusting musical moments in anybody's theatre-going lifetime. Leslie Bricusse and Anthony Newley contributed two first rate numbers in "What Kind Of Fool Am I" and "Who Can I Turn To" (I still think "Whom Can I Turn To" would have been just as big a hit). And who can forget Barbra Streisand singing "People" in FUNNY GIRL? Nevertheless, only in one show that followed FIDDLER could the echoes of the belle epoque be heard and that was MAN OF LA MANCHA in 1965. None of the others, either in aspiration or execution, depth or size, belongs in the league with those post-OKLAHOMA musicals that carried the lyric theatre to its height. Coming as it did as the end of the cycle, somehow it seems only right that FIDDLER should have become the longest running musical of them all.

Since the mid-sixties, the musical theatre has been fumbling, stumbling and groping for the right direction, not certain whether rock is genuine nourishment or merely intravenous feeding. In or out of theatre, rock is primitive stuff, extremely limited dramatically, popularized by the young for the young. Although youth has many glories, it has never been a period distinguished for judgment and that is no less true today. What has misled many who should know better is the vastness of the young population and the vastness of their attendant purchasing power, the two together creating an impression of an important new sound instead of just a loud one. Increasing the volume will never turn a belch into an aria.

Despite the above comments, however, there have been a few successful and exciting rock musicals, notably GOD-SPELL, which used it in a modified form, and JESUS CHRIST, SUPERSTAR, both of which are represented in this volume.

What lies ahead for the musical theatre? That is a question that cannot be answered by the musical theatre alone. Like any other art form, the musical does not exist in a cultural DMZ, but is influenced by and is an expression of its time. Inflation, apathy, the migration of the traditional theatre audience to the suburbs, the fear of the city after dark are but a few of the sociological diseases that have taken it from its historical home on Broadway and put it in the hospital. This is not to say, however, that the theatre, both musical and legitimate, does not have a few nasty problems of its own. It most certainly does. We have, for instance, been living through a period when the gifted beginner has been so overpraised that it has deprived him of the incentive to grow and learn his craft; and the professional has been so scorned that he has become fearful of picking up a pen. But far more dangerous than all that, is the constant and continuing cry: We must attract the youth! Will the young people like it? To me, this is commercialism of the crassest and dumbest variety. What kind of theatre would we have today if Shakespeare had aspired to please the immature? What kind of music would Gershwin have composed if his aim was to delight adolescents? The theatre is, or should be, a mature experience, be it tragic or gay, comedic, farcical, musical or poetic. It is not for the young. Nor is it for the old. It is not even for everybody. It is for people who like the theatre, whatever their age, who go to be transported or amused or uplifted or moved or enchanted on the highest-possible level, the level that has made the theatre survive the ages.

I am convinced that the audience for genuine theatre is still there waiting and wanting to be seduced again, in spite of inflation, apathy and all other sociological ills. Because I believe that and believe it deeply, I cannot be pessimistic about the future.

Besides, if musicals disappeared, what would I do with myself? Eh?

Centre Island, N.Y.

Alan Jay Lerner
February, 1973

Alan Jay Lerner

Jule Styne

Jule Styne: Introduction

The great music and lyrics of the Broadway musical comedy or musical drama have made history not only for their creators, but also for those performers who introduced a song or lyric and subsequently became stars. In fact, composers and lyricists have probably contributed to the making of stars more than almost any other individual creative group.

The reason for this is that theatrical composers and lyricists do not merely write a beautiful popular ballad or a great comedy song. They are (at the very same time) contributing a drama to the play or plays in which they appear. Because of this intermingling of music and drama, a show song has a special feel that makes us remember that moment the rest of our lives. Thus, these songs have fashioned our lives and our children's lives while also fashioning the fever and joy of our country and the world.

Who are some of these great composers and lyricists? Cole Porter, Noel Coward, George Gershwin, Jerome Kern, Kurt Weill, Richard Rodgers, and Frank Loesser, who started me off as a composer. In addition, there are the newer talents that have followed through in the same dramatic professional manner — Stephen Sondheim, Jerry Bock, Sheldon Harnick, Alan Jay Lerner, Fritz Loewe, and . . . Okay, Jule Styne (I wasn't going to include myself, but my ego just whispered "Don't be so modest.")

These men listed above are, first of all, songwriters. However, there are songwriters and then there are songwriters. The talented pop songwriters who mainly write songs for a publisher and/or a record company in order to have hits on the so-called "Top Forty" Billboard and Cash Box charts comprise another type of machinery. I'm not putting this down! I love some of the new words and sounds. However, there are certain new record "sounds" being produced today that, although very brilliant, don't belong in the theatre. Writing show scores is a special and different creativity that you either have or you don't. Show writers are dramatists. They are astute, well-informed students of the theatre, able to be part of a collaborative effort that results in a finished musical comedy. "It ain't easy!"

The musical comedy composer and lyricist know how to further the plot, help develop characters, and above all, be entertaining at the same time. For example, in creating a song for a show, a less theatrically knowledgeable writer will make it so specific that it becomes a bore as entertainment and really does nothing for an audience. Then there are songs that originated as integral parts of a plot but have been performed out of context in clubs all over the world with huge success.

All these songs and thousands of others written by "musical dramatists" are timeless. That is why the theatre and its music have survived over sixty years in our country. Furthermore, the theatre — especially the musical theatre — will always last and flourish because it is the only medium in which an author can express himself without the censorship that is so evident in the confines of most movies and certainly television. Although our country has contributed very little originality to the arts, it has produced some unique musical forms such as the blues, jazz, and that special institution known as the American musical theatre which contains some of the greatest music and live entertainment we have.

Jule Styne
January, 1973

New York, N. Y.

GEORGE GERSHWIN

BETTY COMDEN & ADOLPH GREEN

OSCAR HAMMERSTEIN II & JEROME KERN

RICHARD RODGERS

RICHARD RODGERS & LORENZ HART

KURT WEILL

COLE PORTER

TOM JONES

HARVEY SCHMIDT

10

GEORGE M

NO, NO, NANETTE—Sheet Music Cover

THE BAND WAGON—Sheet Music Cover

From **"Little Johnny Jones"** (1904)

Give My Regards To Broadway

Music & Lyrics by George M. Cohan

Brightly

Verse

1. Did you ev - er see two Yan- kees part up -
2. Say hel - lo to dear old Co - ney Isle, if

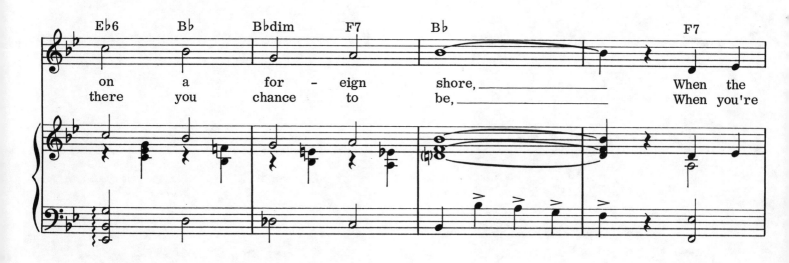

on a for - eign shore, When the
there you chance to be, When you're

Refrain

From "**Little Johnny Jones**" (1904)

Yankee Doodle Dandy

Music & Lyrics by George M. Cohan

Tempo di Marcia

I'm the kid that's all the can-dy, I'm a Yan-kee Doo-dle Dan-dy, I'm glad I
Fa-ther's name was Hez-i-ki-ah, Moth-er's name was Ann Ma-ri-a, Yanks, through and

can you see_____ An-y-thing a-bout a Yan-kee that's a-
can you see_____ An-y-thing a-bout my ped-i-gree that's

phon - ey?
phon - ey?

Interlude

Refrain

Solo

I'm a Yan-kee Doo-dle Dan - dy, A Yan-kee

Doo-dle do or die;_____ A real live neph-ew of my

Un - cle Sam's, Born on the Fourth of Ju - ly. _____ I've

got a Yan-kee Doo-dle sweet - heart, She's my Yan-kee Doo - dle

joy. _____ Yan-kee Doo -dle came to Lon-don, just to ride the po - nies,

I am a Yan-kee Doo-dle boy. _____ boy. _____

19

From **"George White's Scandals"** (1924)

Somebody Loves Me

Lyrics by Ballard Mac·donald & B. G. DeSylva
Music by George Gershwin

From **"No, No, Nanette"** (1925)

Tea For Two

Lyrics by Irving Caesar
Music by Vincent Youmans

Moderato

I'm dis-con-ten-ted with homes that are rent-ed so I have in-ven-ted my own;

Dar-ling, this place is a lov-er's o-a-sis, where life's wea-ry chase is un-

27

From **"No, No, Nanette"** (1925)

I Want To Be Happy

Lyrics by Irving Caesar
Music by Vincent Youmans

Moderato

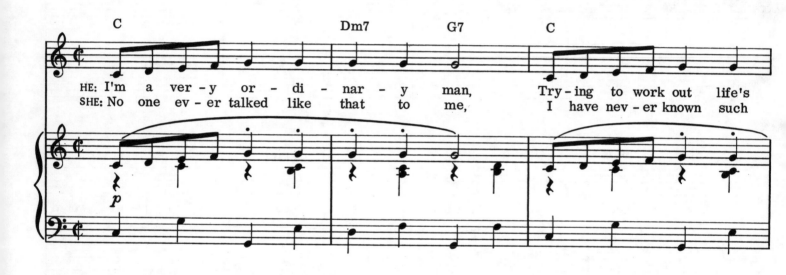

HE: I'm a ver-y or-di-nar-y man, Try-ing to work out life's
SHE: No one ev-er talked like that to me, I have nev-er known such

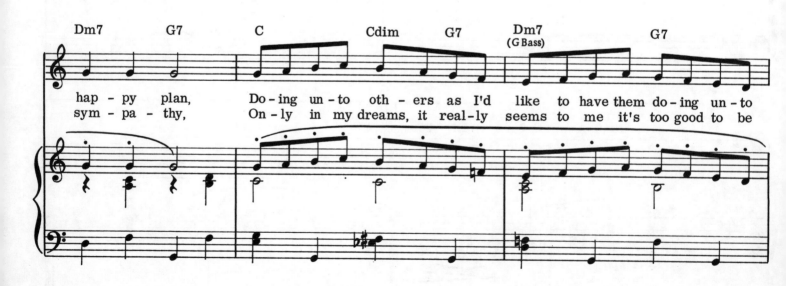

hap-py plan, Do-ing un-to oth-ers as I'd like to have them do-ing un-to
sym-pa-thy, On-ly in my dreams, it real-ly seems to me it's too good to be

Refrain

From **"Oh, Kay"** (1926)

Someone To Watch Over Me

Lyrics by Ira Gershwin
Music by George Gershwin

Refrain

From **"Good News"** (1927)

The Best Things In Life Are Free

Music & Lyrics by B. G. DeSylva, Lew Brown and Ray Henderson

Moderato

From **"A Connecticut Yankee"** (1927)

My Heart Stood Still

Lyrics by Lorenz Hart
Music by Richard Rodgers

Refrain
Slow, but liltingly *(Molto tranquillo)*

41

And then my heart stood still!

My feet could step and walk, My lips could move and talk,

And yet my heart stood still! Though not a

sin - gle word was spo - ken, I could tell you knew,

From **"Follow Thru"** (1929)

Button Up Your Overcoat

Music & Lyrics by B. G. DeSylva, Lew Brown and Ray Henderson

Lis - ten, Big Boy!___ Now that I've got you made,
Lis - ten, Girl friend!___ You've knocked me off my feet.

Good-ness, but I'm a - fraid Some-thing's gon - na hap-pen to you.
I think you're ver - y sweet Mak - ing such a fuss a - bout me.

From **"The Little Show"** (1929)

I Guess I'll Have To Change My Plan

Lyrics by Howard Dietz
Music by Arthur Schwartz

51

From "**The Band Wagon**" (1931)

Dancing In The Dark

Lyrics by Howard Dietz
Music by Arthur Schwartz

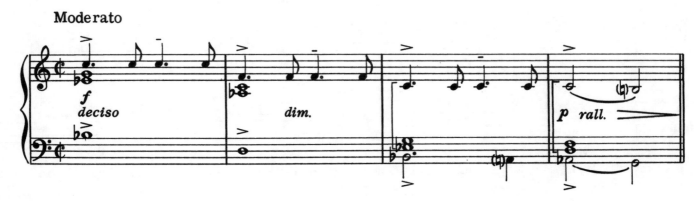

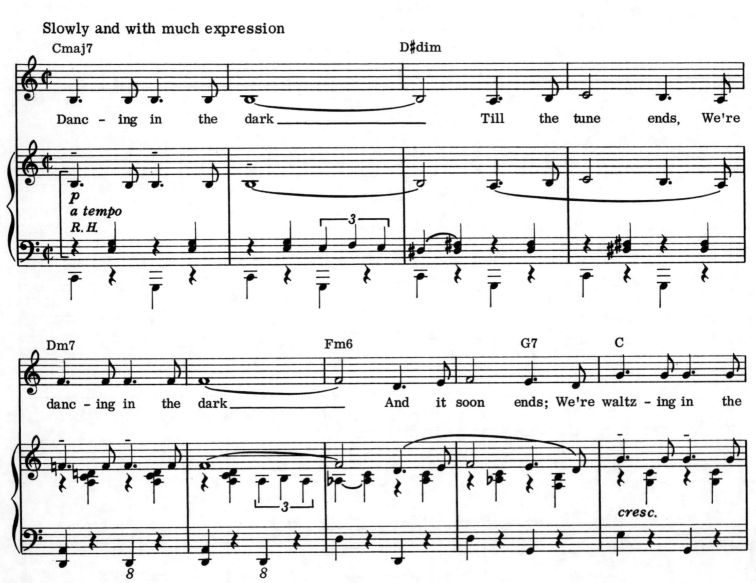

wonder of why we're here._____ Time hurries by, we're here_____ and gone Looking for the light_____ Of a new love to brighten up the night,_____ I have you, love, And we can face the music togeth -

53

56

From **"Gay Divorce"** (1932)

Night And Day

Music & Lyrics by Cole Porter

58

61

From **"Roberta"** (1933)

Smoke Gets In Your Eyes

Lyrics by Otto Harbach
Music by Jerome Kern

nied._____ They said some-day you'll

find All who love are blind,_____ When your heart's on

fire, You must re-al - ize Smoke gets in your eyes._____

Un poco più mosso

So I chaffed____ them and I gay-ly laughed____ to think they could doubt my

63

From **"Conversation Piece"** (1934)

I'll Follow My Secret Heart

Music & Lyrics by Noël Coward

No mat-ter what price is paid, What stars may fade a-bove,_____ I'll fol-low my se-cret heart till I find love._____ love._____

69

You're The Top

Music & Lyrics by Cole Porter

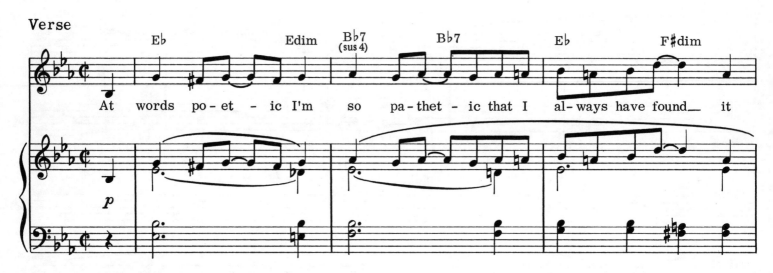

Verse

At words po-et-ic I'm so pa-thet-ic that I al-ways have found it

best,_____ In-stead of get-ting 'em off__ my chest,_____ to let 'em

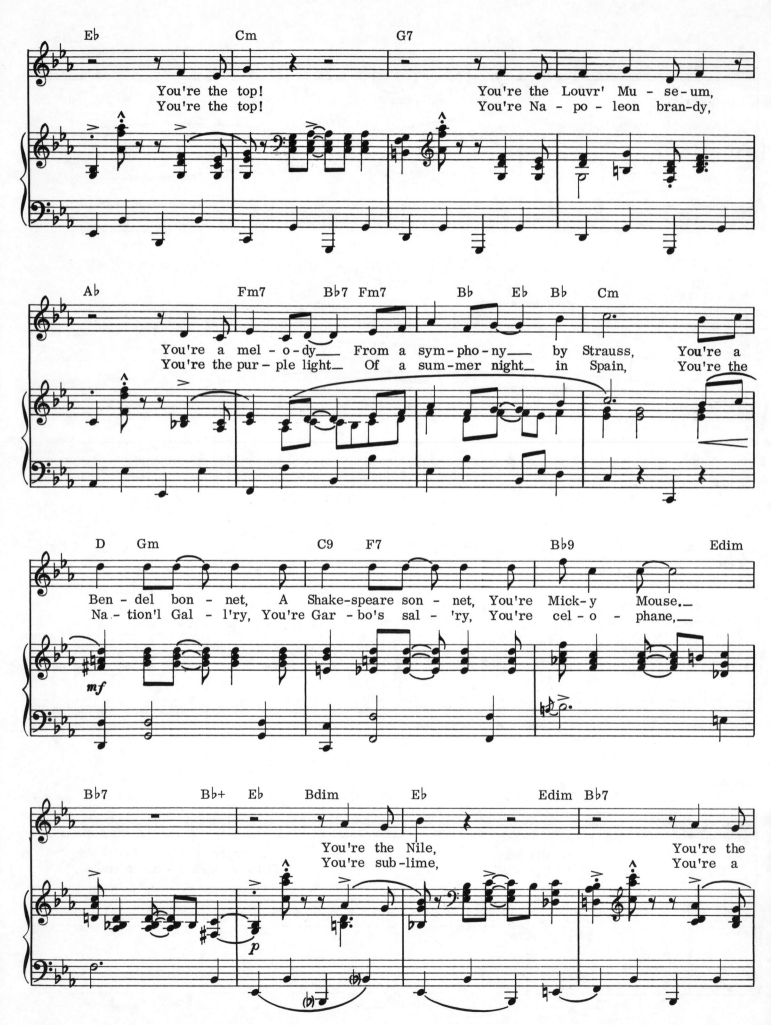

Tow'r of Pi - sa,
tur - key din - ner,
You're the smile on the
You're the time of the

Mo - na Lis - a;
Der - by win - ner,
I'm a worth-less check,— a to - tal wreck,— a
I'm a toy bal-loon— that is fat - ed soon— to

flop,
pop;
But if Ba - by, I'm— the bot-tom, You're— the

top!

top!

From **"Porgy And Bess"** (1935)

Summertime

Lyrics by DuBose Heyward
Music by George Gershwin

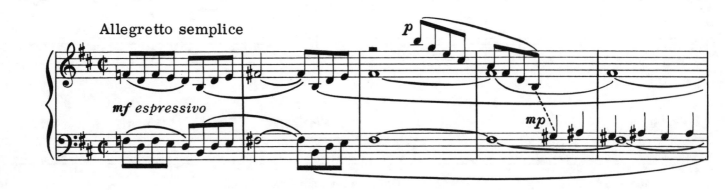

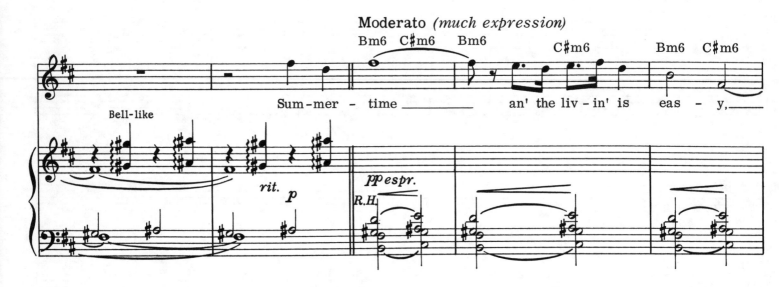

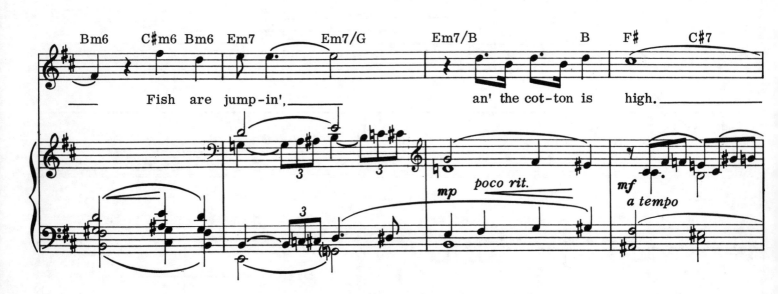

From **"Jubilee"** (1935)

Begin The Beguine

Music & Lyrics by Cole Porter

mem - ber____ When they be - gin____ the Be-

guine.____ Oh, yes, let them be-gin the Be - guine, make them

play____ Till the stars that were there be-fore re-turn a -

bove you,____ Till you whis-per to me once more, "Dar-ling, I

From **"Jubilee"** (1935)

Just One Of Those Things

Music & Lyrics by Cole Porter

Allegretto

As Dor-o-thy Par - ker once said _____ to her boy - friend, _____

_____ "Fare thee well," _____ As Col - um - bus an - nounced _ when he

Refrain

It was just one____ of those things,_____ Just one____ of those cra - zy flings.__ One of those bells that now and then rings, Just one____ of those things._____ It was just one____ of those nights,_____ Just one____ of those fab - u - lous

86

to cool down._____ So good-bye, dear,_ and A-

men,_____ Here's hop - ing we meet now and then,_

___ It was great fun,_ But it was just one_ of those

things._____

1. It was

2.

From **"Red, Hot And Blue"** (1936)

It's De-lovely

Music & Lyrics by Cole Porter

HE: I feel a sud-den urge to sing,__ The kind of dit-ty that in-vokes the Spring,__ So con-trol your de-sire to curse while I cru-ci-fy the

Refrain

Very rhythmically

The night is young,___ The skies are clear___ And if you want___ to go walk-ing, dear,___ It's de-light-ful,___ it's de-li-cious,___ it's de-love-ly.___ I un-der-stand___ the rea-son why___ You're sen-ti-men-tal, 'cause so am I,___ It's de-

*Pronounced "delukes."

From **"On Your Toes"** (1936)

There's A Small Hotel

Lyrics by Lorenz Hart
Music by Richard Rodgers

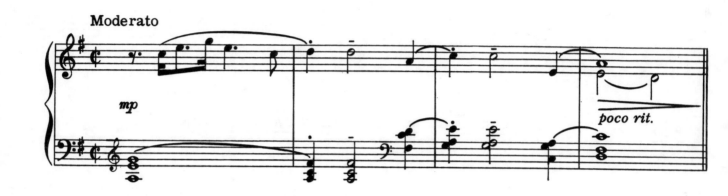

Refrain

From **"Ziegfeld Follies of 1936"**

I Can't Get Started

Lyrics by Ira Gershwin
Music by Vernon Duke

All the pa - pers where I led the news With my ca - pers now will spread the news,

"Su - per - man Turns Out To Be Flash In The Pan!"

Refrain

1. I've flown a - round the world in a plane; I've set - tled re - vo - lu - tions in
2. (I do a) hun - dred yards in ten flat; The Prince of Wales has cop - ied my

Spain; The North Pole I have char - ted, But can't get start - ed with
hat; With queens I've à la cart - ed, But can't get start - ed with

From **"Babes In Arms"** (1937)

My Funny Valentine

Lyrics by Lorenz Hart
Music by Richard Rodgers

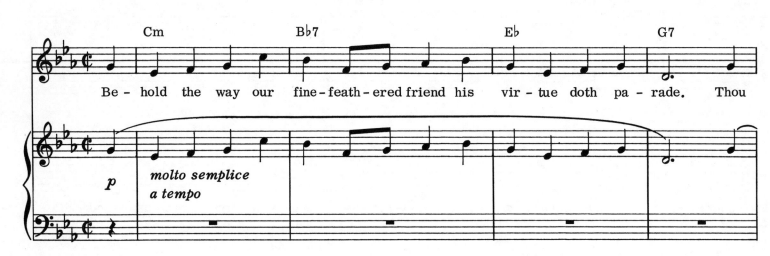

Be - hold the way our fine - feath - ered friend his vir - tue doth pa - rade. Thou

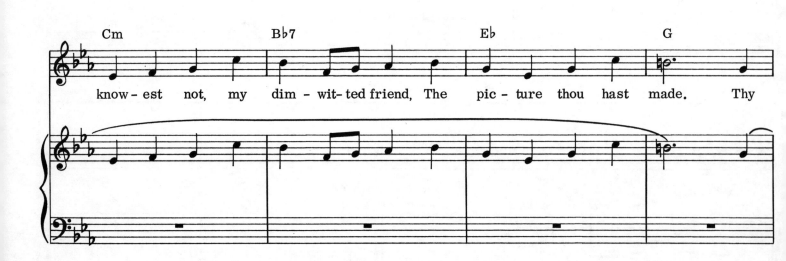

know - est not, my dim - wit - ted friend, The pic - ture thou hast made. Thy

va - cant brow and thy tou - sled hair con - ceal thy good in - tent. Thou

no - ble, up - right, truth - ful, sin - cere and slight - ly dop - ey gent, you're

Refrain-Slowly *(with much expression)*

My fun - ny Val - en - tine, Sweet com - ic

Val - en - tine, You make me smile with my

103

From **"I'd Rather Be Right"** (1937)

Have You Met Miss Jones?

Lyrics by Lorenz Hart
Music by Richard Rodgers

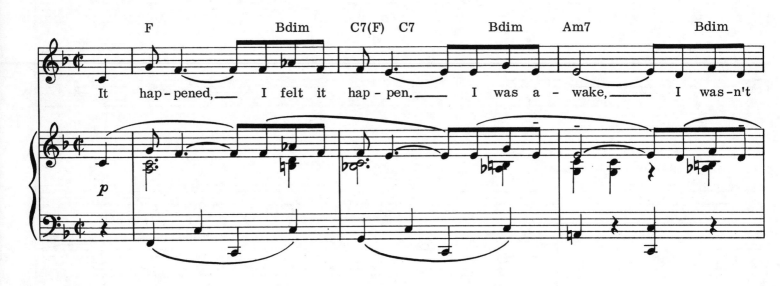

Refrain

Gracefully and not fast

earth and sky!_____

Now I've met Miss Jones, And we'll keep on

meet - ing till we die,_____ Miss Jones and

DuBARRY WAS A LADY

THE BOYS FROM SYRACUSE—Sheet Music Cover

LEAVE IT TO ME

ON YOUR TOES

RED, HOT AND BLUE

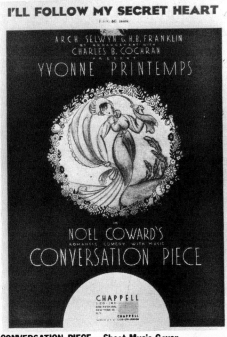

CONVERSATION PIECE—Sheet Music Cover

ROBERTA

ON YOUR TOES—Playbill Cover

From **"The Boys From Syracuse"** (1938)

This Can't Be Love

Lyrics by Lorenz Hart
Music by Richard Rodgers

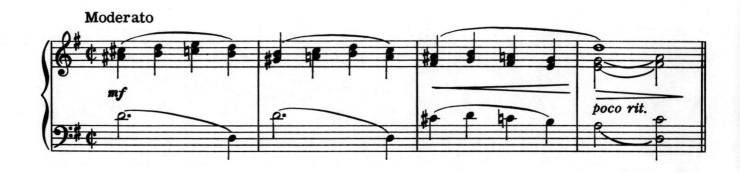

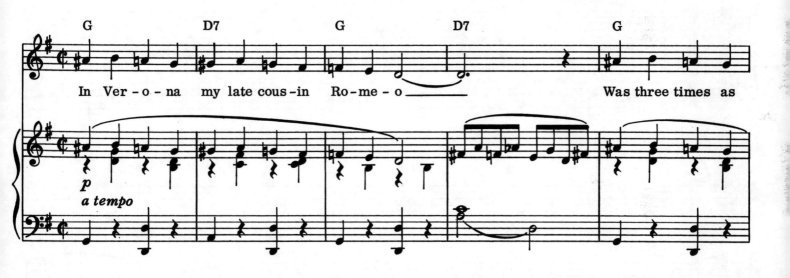

In Ver-o-na my late cous-in Ro-me-o_____ Was three times as

stu-pid as my Drom-i-o._____ For he fell in love and then he

Refrain

This can't be love be - cause I feel so well,____ No
sobs, no sor - rows, no sighs;_____ This can't be
love, I get no diz - zy spell.__ My head is not____ in the

From **"Knickerbocker Holiday"** (1938)

September Song

Lyrics by Maxwell Anderson
Music by Kurt Weill

Moderato assai

G7   Fdim   Am7   Am6   G7   Ddim

When I was a young man court - ing the girls, I played me a wait - ing
(When you) meet with the young men ear - ly in spring, They court you in song and

Am7   Am6   G9   Fdim   Am7   Gdim   Dm6   G9+

game; If a maid re - fused me with toss - ing curls, I let the old earth take a
rhyme, They woo you with words and a clo - ver ring, But if you ex - am - ine the

From **"Leave It To Me"** (1938)

My Heart Belongs To Daddy

Music & Lyrics by Cole Porter

Refrain

Slow Rhumba tempo

119

From **"DuBarry Was A Lady"** (1939)

Friendship

Music & Lyrics by Cole Porter

friend - ship,___ friend - ship,___ Just a per - fect

blend - ship.___ When oth - er friend - ships have

been for - git___ Ours will still be it,___ Lah - dle-

ah - dle - ah - dle, hep, hep, hep.___ If they

From **"Too Many Girls"** (1939)

I Didn't Know What Time It Was

Lyrics by Lorenz Hart
Music by Richard Rodgers

From **"Higher And Higher"** (1940)

It Never Entered My Mind

Lyrics by Lorenz Hart
Music by Richard Rodgers

And now I e-ven have to scratch my back my-self.

Once you warned me That if you scorned me, I'd sing the maid-en's

pray'r a-gain.__ And wish that you were there a-gain__ To get in-to my

hair a-gain,__ It nev-er en-tered my mind.__

From **"Pal Joey"** (1940)

Bewitched

Lyrics by Lorenz Hart
Music by Richard Rodgers

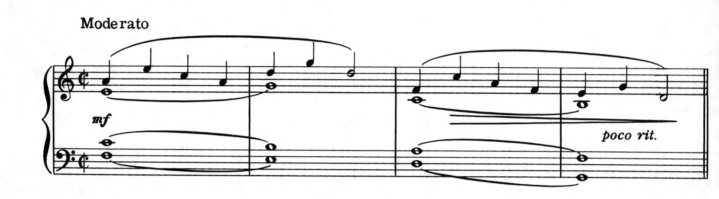

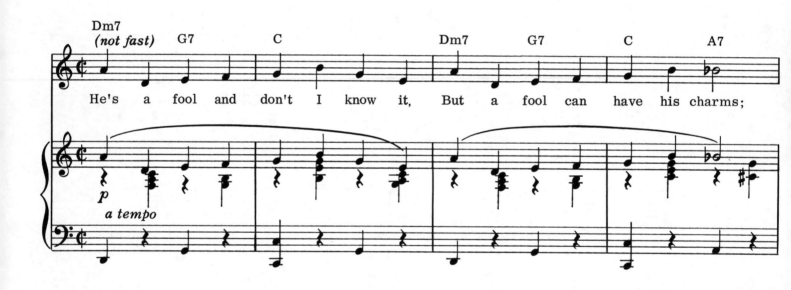

He's a fool and don't I know it, But a fool can have his charms;

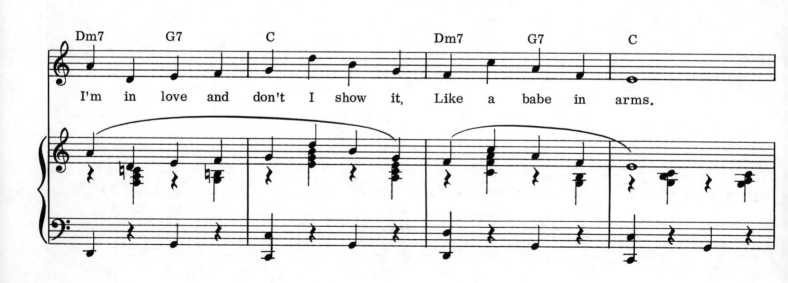

I'm in love and don't I show it, Like a babe in arms.

135

137

From **"Oklahoma!"** (1943)

The Surrey With The Fringe On Top

Lyrics by Oscar Hammerstein II
Music by Richard Rodgers

Brightly

When I take you out, to-night, with me,_____

Hon - ey, here's the way it's goin' to be:_____

weath - er. Two bright side-light's wink-in' and blink-in', Ain't no fin - er
o - ver: Don't you wisht y'd go on for-ev-er? Don't you wisht y'd
med - der. Hush, you bird, my ba-by's a-sleep-in'! May-be got a

rig, I'm a-think-in' You c'n keep your rig if you're think-in' 'at I'd
go on for-ev-er? Don't you wisht y'd go on for-ev-er and ud
dream worth a-keep-in' Whoa! you team, and jist keep a-creep-in' at a

keer to swap Fer that shin-y, lit-tle sur-rey with the fringe on the
nev - er stop In that shin-y, lit-tle sur-rey with the fringe on the
slow clip clop. Don't you hur-ry with the sur-rey with the fringe on the

1. 2.
top!
top!

3.
top! _____

141

From **"Oklahoma!"** (1943)

Oh, What A Beautiful Mornin'

Lyrics by Oscar Hammerstein II
Music by Richard Rodgers

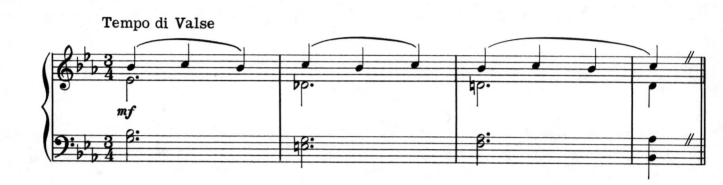

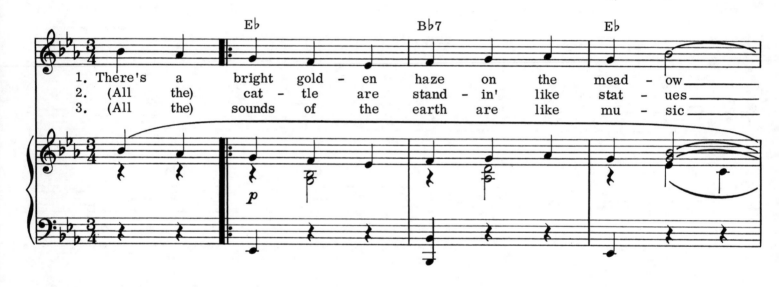

1. There's a bright gold - en haze on the mead - ow___
2. (All the) cat - tle are stand - in' like stat - ues___
3. (All the) sounds of the earth are like mu - sic___

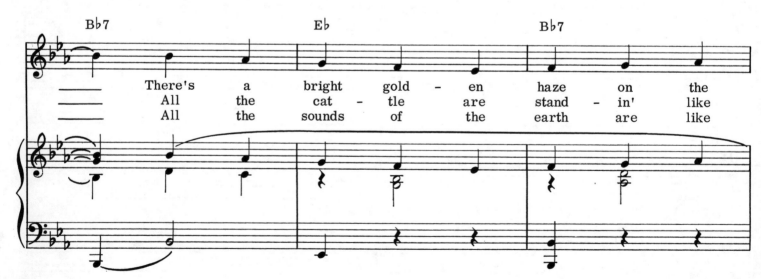

___ There's a bright gold - en haze on the
___ All the cat - tle are stand - in' like
___ All the sounds of the earth are like

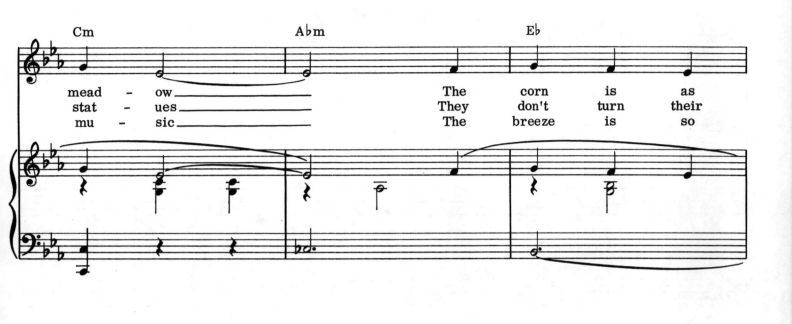

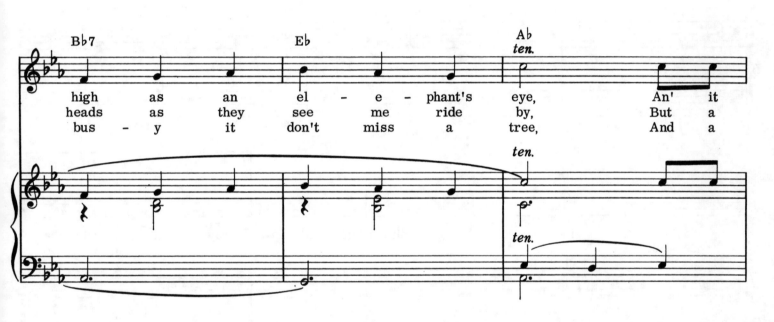

Refrain

From **"Carousel"** (1945)

If I Loved You

Lyrics by Oscar Hammerstein II
Music by Richard Rodgers

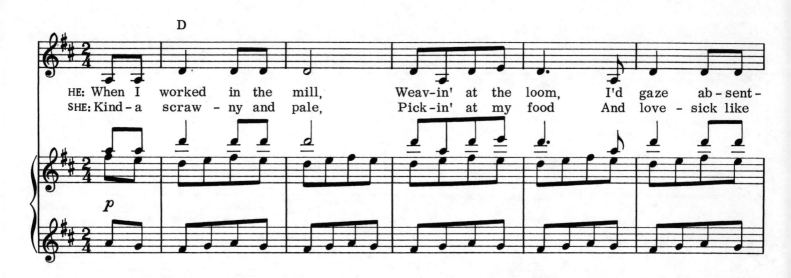

HE: When I worked in the mill, Weav-in' at the loom, I'd gaze ab-sent-
SHE: Kind-a scraw-ny and pale, Pick-in' at my food And love-sick like

mind-ed at the roof _____ And half the time the shut-tle 'd
an-y oth-er guy _____ I'd throw a-way my sweat-er and

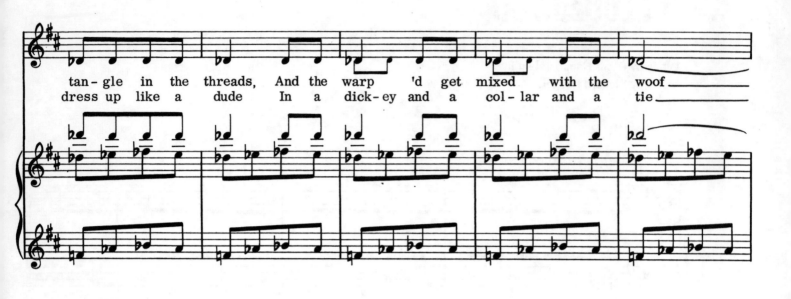

tan - gle in the threads, And the warp 'd get mixed with the woof _____
dress up like a dude In a dick-ey and a col - lar and a tie _____

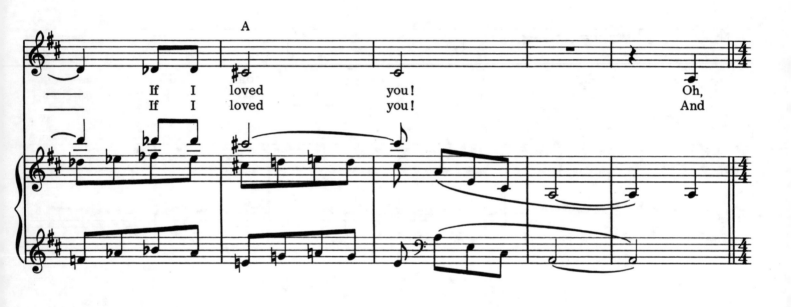

If I loved you!
If I loved you!

Oh,
And

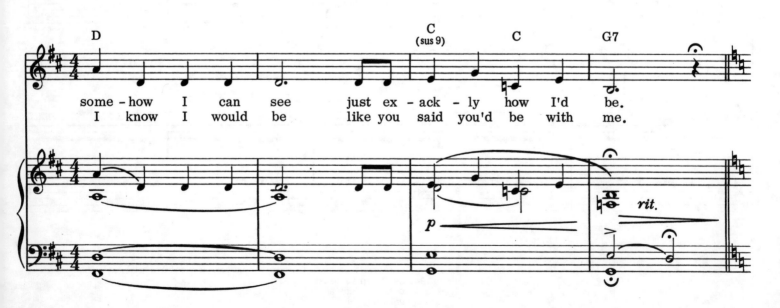

some - how I can see just ex - ack - ly how I'd be.
I know I would be like you said you'd be with me.

Refrain

With great warmth and slowly

If I loved you, Time and a-gain I would
try to say All I'd want you to
know. If I loved you,
Words would-n't come in an eas-y way, 'Round in

148

From **"Carousel"** (1945)

You'll Never Walk Alone

Lyrics by Oscar Hammerstein II
Music by Richard Rodgers

152

From **"Brigadoon"** (1947)

Almost Like Being In Love

Lyrics by Alan Jay Lerner
Music by Frederick Loewe

Refrain

What a day this has been! What a rare mood I'm in! Why, it's al-most like be-ing in love. There's a smile on my face for the whole hu-man race, Why, it's al-most like be-ing in love! All the mu-sic of life seems to

154

From **"Finian's Rainbow"** (1947)

How Are Things In Glocca Morra?

Lyrics by E. Y. Harburg
Music by Burton Lane

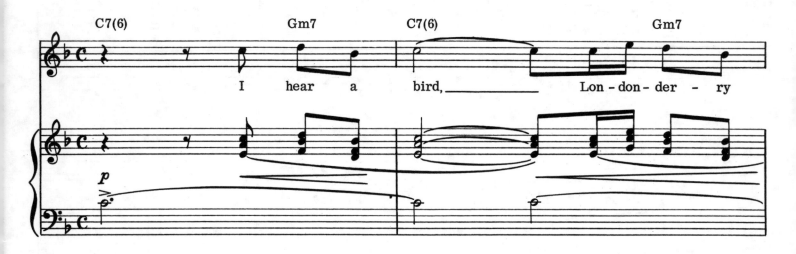

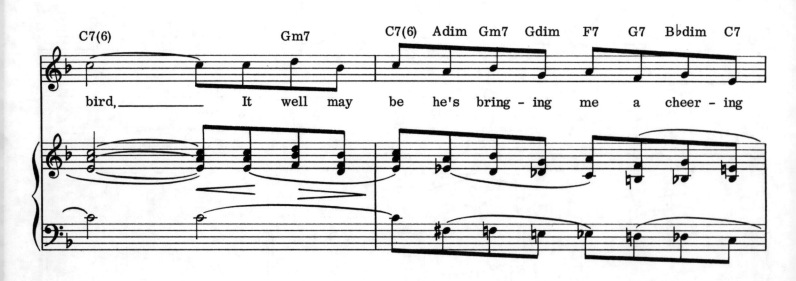

From "**Kiss Me, Kate**" (1948)

Wunderbar

Music & Lyrics by Cole Porter

Refrain

bar! _____ Wun - der - bar, _____ wun - der - bar! _____

_____ We're a - lone and hand in glove, _____ Not a

cloud near or far, _____ Why, it's

more than wun - der - bar! _____ Oh, I

From **"South Pacific"** (1949)

Some Enchanted Evening

Lyrics by Oscar Hammerstein II
Music by Richard Rodgers

Fools give you rea - sons, Wise men nev - er try.

Some en - chant - ed eve - ning

When you find your true love, When you feel her call you

A - cross a crowd - ed room, Then fly to her

168

From **"South Pacific"** (1949)

Younger Than Springtime

Lyrics by Oscar Hammerstein II
Music by Richard Rodgers

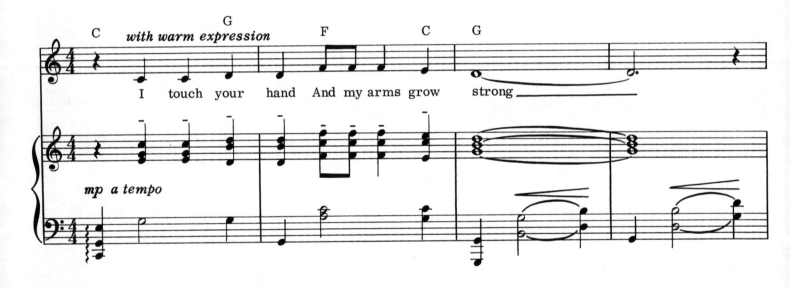

I touch your hand And my arms grow strong

Like a pair of birds That burst with song.

From **"The King And I"** (1951)

Hello, Young Lovers

Lyrics by Oscar Hammerstein II
Music by Richard Rodgers

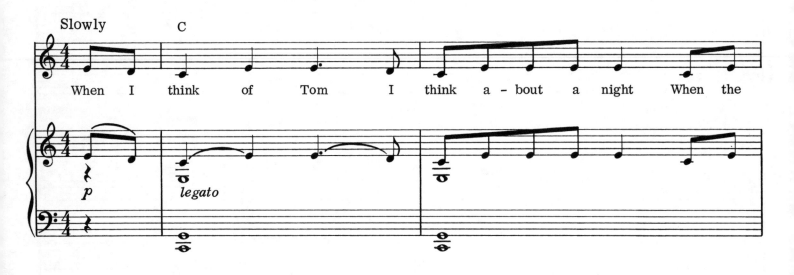

Refrain
Very moderately

Hel - lo, young lov - ers, Who - ev - er you are, I hope your trou - bles are few All my good wish - es go with you to - night I've been in love like

you _____ Be brave, young lov - ers, and fol - low your

star, Be brave and faith - ful and true _____

Cling ver - y close to each oth - er to - night I've been in

love like you. _____ I know how it feels to have

From **"Paint Your Wagon"** (1951)

They Call The Wind Maria

Lyrics by Alan Jay Lerner
Music by Frederick Loewe

Vivo, ben marcato

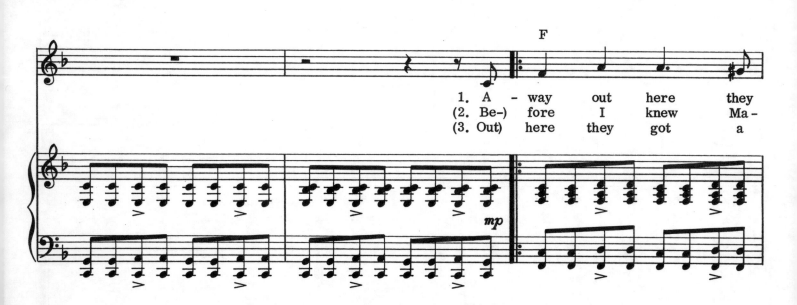

1. A - way   out   here   they
(2. Be-) fore   I   knew   Ma - a
(3. Out) here   they   got   a

got a name For rain, and wind, and fi - re. The
ri - a's name And heard her wail and whin - in'. I
name for rain, For wind and fi - re on - ly. But

rain is Tess, the fi - re's Jo, And they call the wind Ma -
had a girl, and she had me, And the sun was al - ways
when you're lost, and all a - lone, There ain't no word but

ri - a.* Ma - ri - a blows the stars a - round, And
shin - in'. But then one day I left my girl, I
lone - ly. And I'm a lost and lone - ly man, With-

sends the clouds a - fly - in'. Ma - ri - a makes the
left her far be - hind me. And now I'm lost, so
out a star to guide me. Ma - ri - a, blow my

*pronounced "Ma-rye-a"

181

From **"Can-Can"** (1953)

I Love Paris

Music & Lyrics by Cole Porter

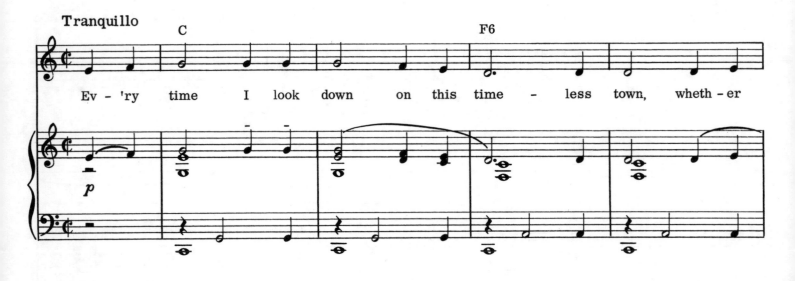

Refrain

Slow Fox-trot tempo

185

From **"Me And Juliet"** (1953)

No Other Love

Lyrics by Oscar Hammerstein II
Music by Richard Rodgers

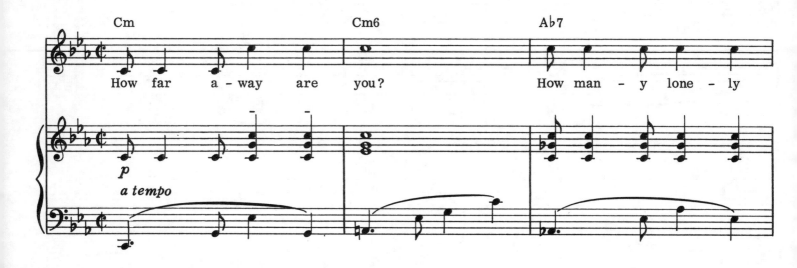

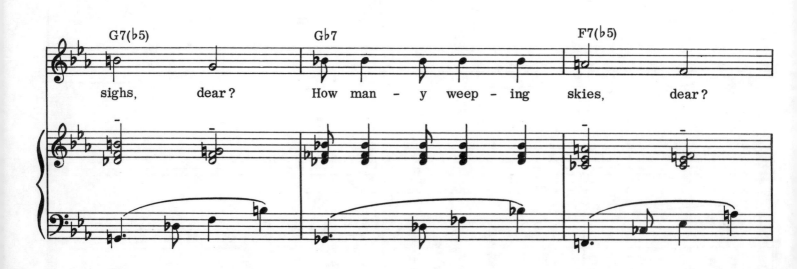

Refrain
Slow Tango tempo

190

From **"Silk Stockings"** (1955)

All Of You

Music & Lyrics by Cole Porter

Fox trot tempo

(with a bounce, but not too fast)

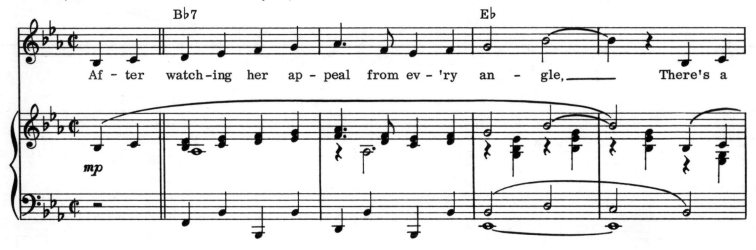

Af - ter watch-ing her ap-peal from ev-'ry an - gle,_____ There's a

big ro - man - tic deal I've got to wan - gle._____ For I've

even the heart and soul of you. So love, at least, a small per-cent of me, do, For I love all of you. I love the you. you.

From **"Bells Are Ringing"** (1956)

Just In Time

Lyrics by Betty Comden & Adolph Green
Music by Jule Styne

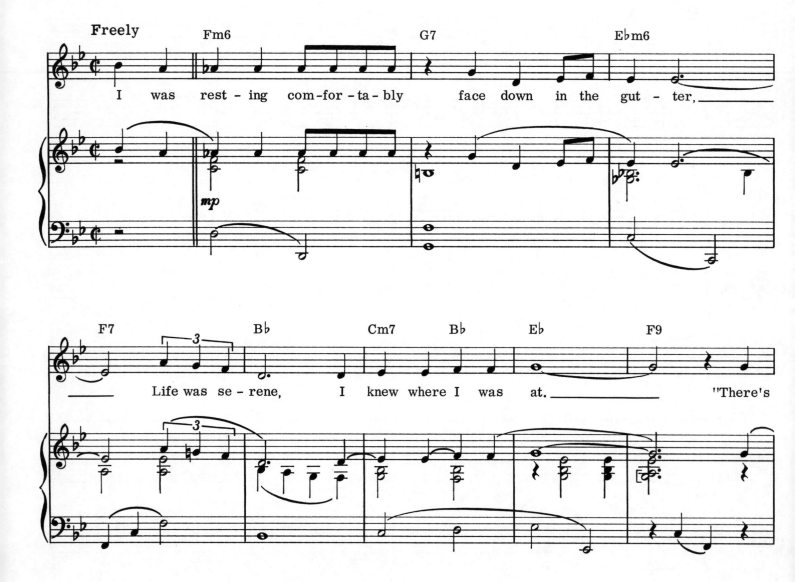

Refrain

With a lilt

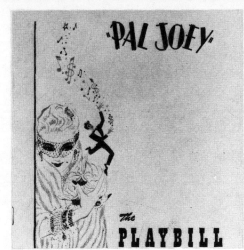

PAL JOEY—Playbill Cover

OKLAHOMA! — Showcard

CAROUSEL

BRIGADOON—Sheet Music Cover

KISS ME, KATE

SOUTH PACIFIC

THE KING AND I

ME AND JULIET — Playbill Cover

CAN—CAN

BELLS ARE RINGING — Playbill Cover

MY FAIR LADY

THE SOUND OF MUSIC

From **"Bells Are Ringing"** (1956)

The Party's Over

Lyrics by Betty Comden & Adolph Green
Music by Jule Styne

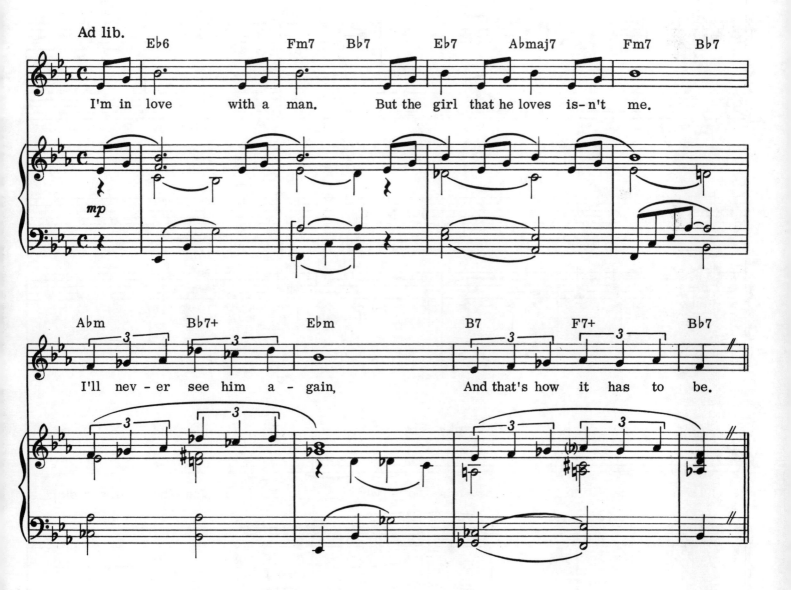

Refrain

With feeling

The par-ty's o-ver,_____ It's time to call it a day._____ They've burst your pret-ty bal-loon and tak-en the moon a-way._____ It's time to wind up_____ the mas-quer-ade._____ Just make your mind up_____ The pi-per must be paid. The par-ty's o-ver,_____ The can-dles flick-er and dim.

From **"My Fair Lady"** (1956)

On The Street Where You Live

Lyrics by Alan Jay Lerner
Music by Frederick Loewe

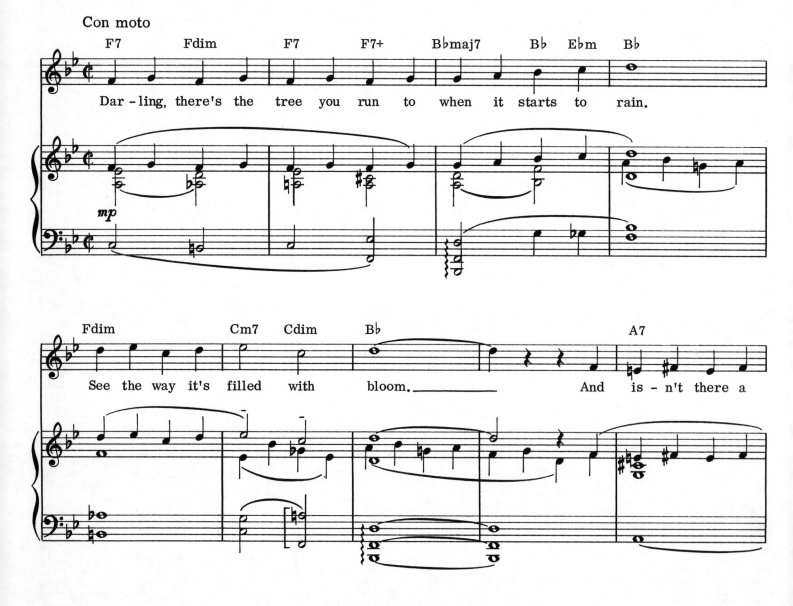

From **"My Fair Lady"** (1956)

I Could Have Danced All Night

Lyrics by Alan Jay Lerner
Music by Frederick Loewe

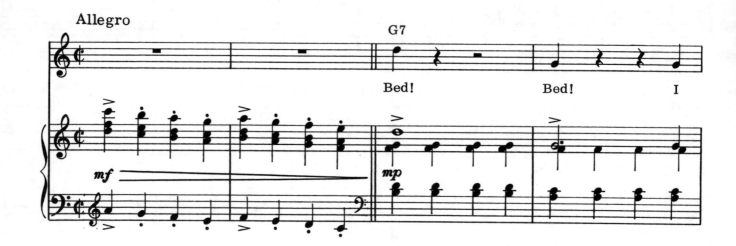

when he _____ be-gan to dance _____ with

me, _____ I could have danced, danced, danced, _____

All night. I could have night. _____

From **"West Side Story"** (1957)

Tonight

Lyrics by Stephen Sondheim
Music by Leonard Bernstein

From **"The Sound Of Music"** (1959)

Climb Ev'ry Mountain

Lyrics by Oscar Hammerstein II
Music by Richard Rodgers

Refrain

(with deep feeling, like a prayer)

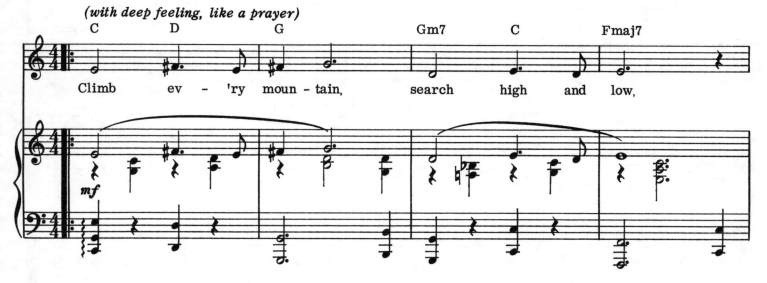

Climb ev - 'ry moun - tain, search high and low,

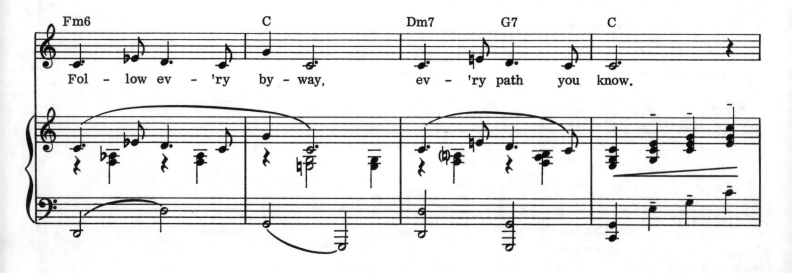

Fol - low ev - 'ry by - way, ev - 'ry path you know.

220

From **"Camelot"** (1960)

Camelot

Lyrics by Alan Jay Lerner
Music by Frederick Loewe

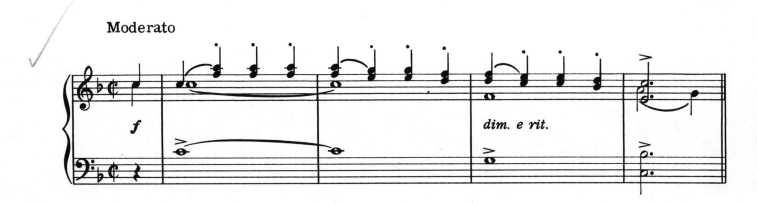

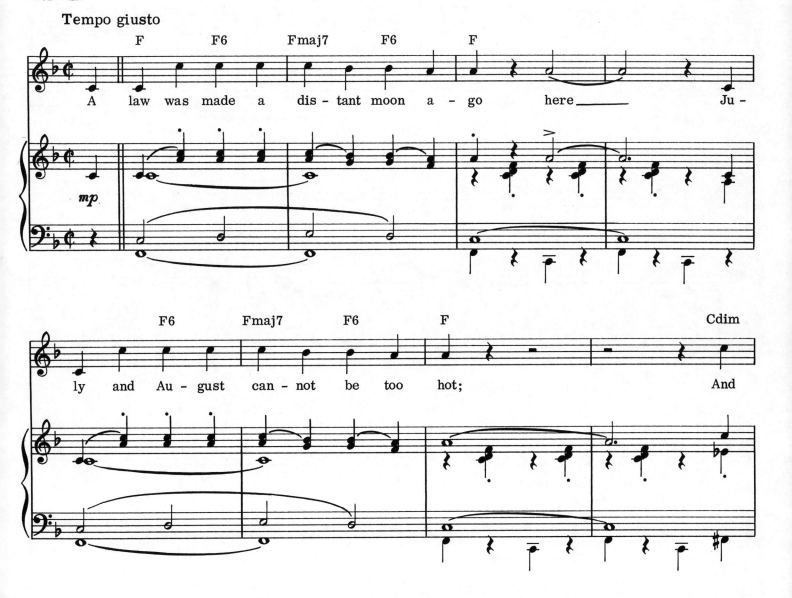

there's a le - gal lim - it to the snow here_____ In

Cam - e - lot. The

win - ter is for - bid - den till De - cem - ber_____ And

ex - its March the sec - ond on the dot. By

or - der sum - mer lin - gers through Sep - tem - ber _____ in

Cam - e - lot.

Cam - e - lot!   Cam - e -lot!   I know it
Cam - e - lot!   Cam - e -lot!   I know it

sounds a bit bi - zarre,   But in
gives a per - son pause,   But in

223

From **"Camelot"** (1960)

I Loved You Once In Silence

Lyrics by Alan Jay Lerner
Music by Frederick Loewe

Refrain

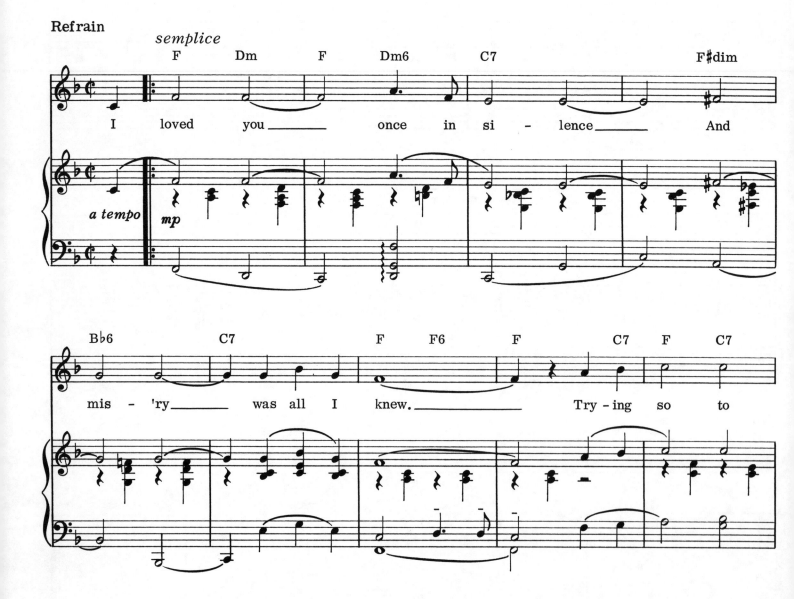

228

door. _____ Ev-'ry joy - ous word of love was spo - ken.

And now there's twice as much grief, Twice the strain for us; Twice the de -
And af - ter all had been said, Here we are, my love, Si - lent once

spair, Twice the pain for us As we had known be -
more, And not far, my love, From where we were be -

1.
fore. _____ I

2.
fore. _____

From "**Camelot**" (1960)

If Ever I Would Leave You

Lyrics by Alan Jay Lerner
Music by Frederick Loewe

Refrain

From **"Wildcat"** (1960)

Hey Look Me Over

Lyrics by Carolyn Leigh
Music by Cy Coleman

March tempo

mf *sf*

Refrain

G   B7   F#m7   Ddim   B7

mp - mf   (Opt.)

Hey, look me o - ver, lend me an ear;

E7   Am

Fresh out of clo - ver, mort - gaged up to here._____ But

don't pass the plate, folks, don't pass the cup; _____ I

fig - ure when - ev - er you're down and out, the on - ly way is

up. And I'll be up like a rose - bud, high on the

vine; Don't thumb your nose, bud, take a tip from

235

From **"Do Re Mi"** (1960)

Make Someone Happy

Lyrics by Betty Comden & Adolph Green
Music by Jule Styne

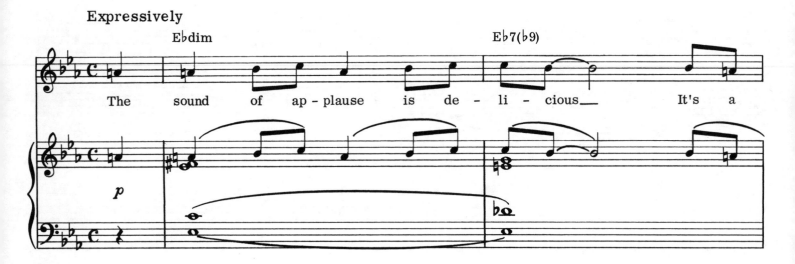

The sound of ap-plause is de-li-cious— It's a

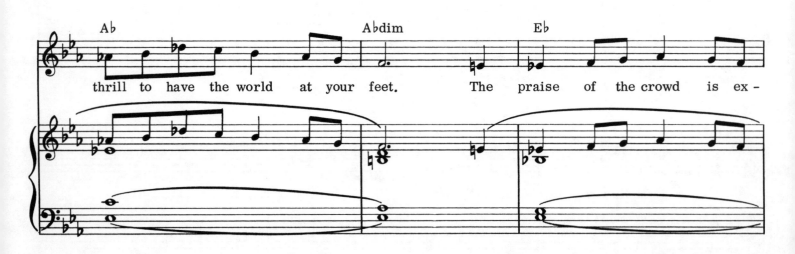

thrill to have the world at your feet. The praise of the crowd is ex-

From **"Bye Bye Birdie"** (1960)

Put On A Happy Face

Lyrics by Lee Adams
Music by Charles Strouse

From **"The Fantasticks"** (1960)

Try To Remember

Lyrics by Tom Jones
Music by Harvey Schmidt

Moderato

Refrain

Slowly, with tenderness

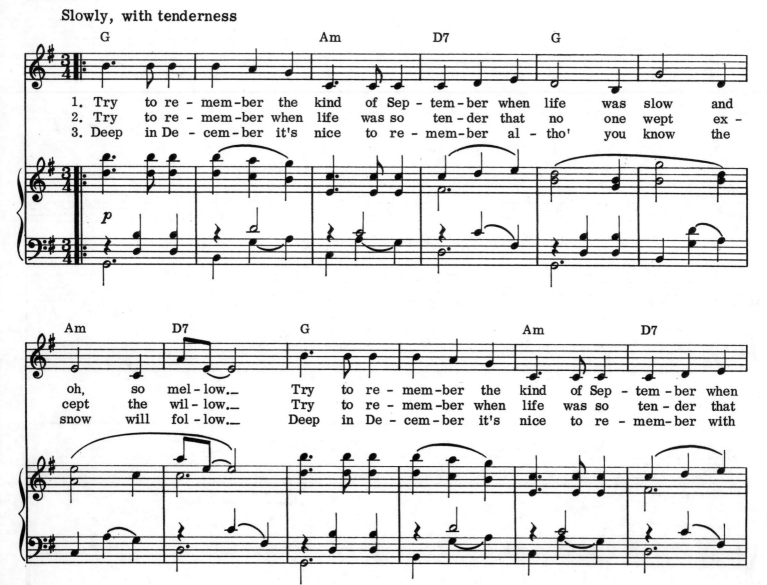

1. Try to re-mem-ber the kind of Sep-tem-ber when life was slow and
2. Try to re-mem-ber when life was so ten-der that no one wept ex-
3. Deep in De-cem-ber it's nice to re-mem-ber al-tho' you know the

oh, so mel-low.— Try to re-mem-ber the kind of Sep-tem-ber when
cept the wil-low.— Try to re-mem-ber when life was so ten-der that
snow will fol-low.— Deep in De-cem-ber it's nice to re-mem-ber with

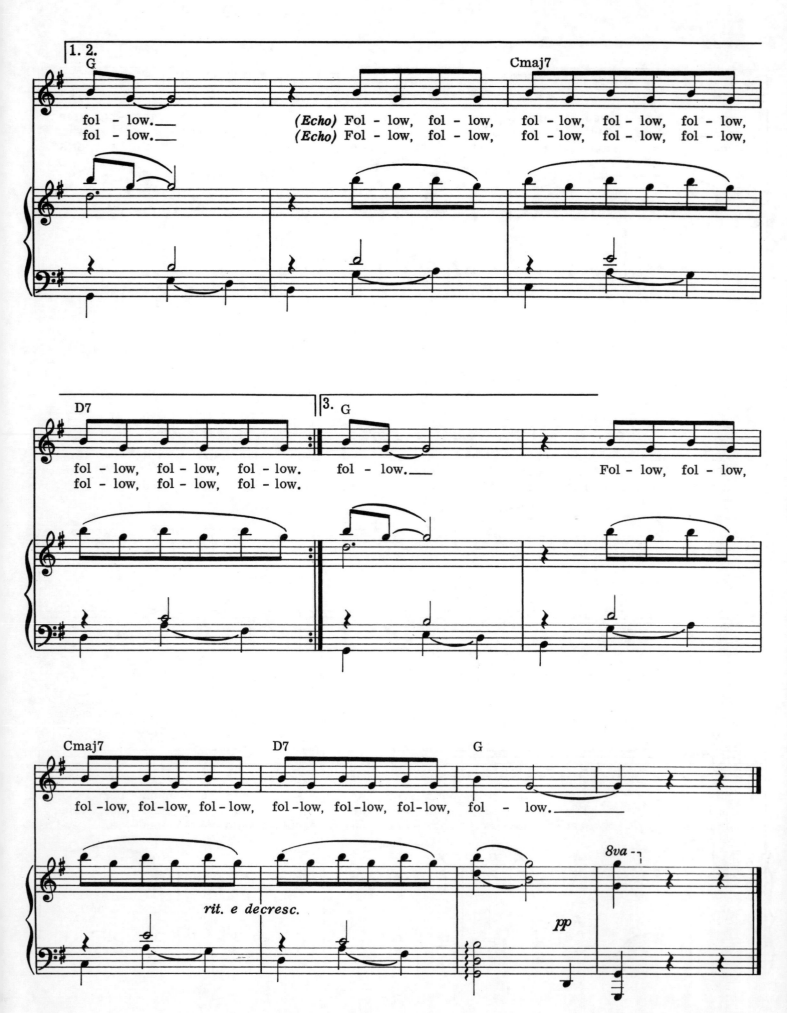

From "**Stop The World I Want To Get Off**" (1962)

What Kind Of Fool Am I?

Music & Lyrics by Leslie Bricusse and Anthony Newley

Moderately slow

What kind of fool am I?_____ Who nev - er fell in love,____

_ It seems that I'm the on - ly one that I have been

From **"She Loves Me"** (1963)

She Loves Me

Lyrics by Sheldon Harnick
Music by Jerry Bock

Well, well, well, well, well, well, well,

well, well, well,_____ will won - ders nev - er cease?

Chorus — Moderately bright

From "Hello, Dolly!" (1964)

Hello, Dolly!

Music & Lyrics by Jerry Herman

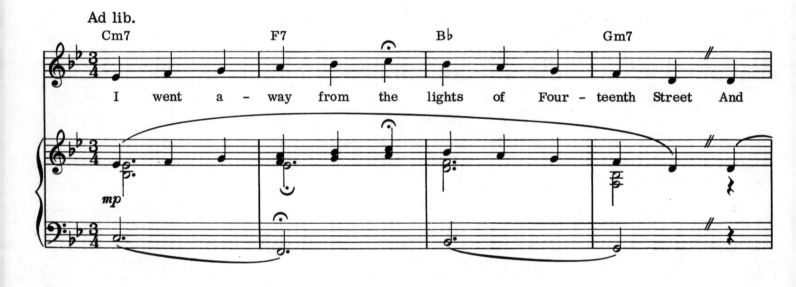

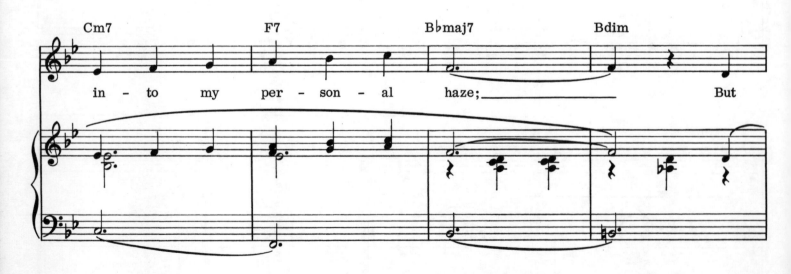

From **"Funny Girl"** (1964)

People

Lyrics by Bob Merrill
Music by Jule Styne

From **"Fiddler On The Roof"** (1964)

Sunrise, Sunset

Lyrics by Sheldon Harnick
Music by Jerry Bock

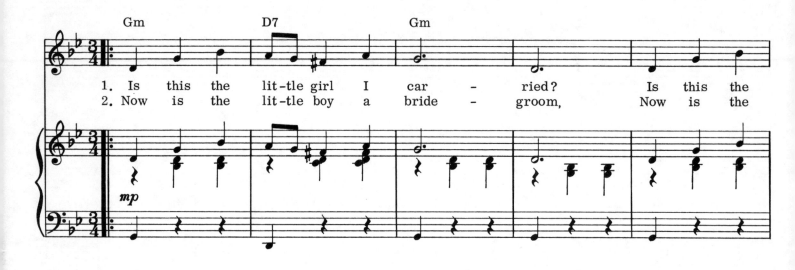

1. Is this the lit-tle girl I car - ried? Is this the
2. Now is the lit-tle boy a bride - groom, Now is the

lit-tle boy at play?   I don't re - mem-ber grow-ing
lit-tle girl a bride.   Un - der the can - o - py I

Chorus

Sun - rise,____ Sun - set, Sun - rise,____ Sun - set,

Swift - ly____ flow the days;____ Seed - lings turn

o - ver - night to sun - flow'rs, Blos - som - ing e - ven as we

gaze.____ Sun - rise,____ Sun - set,

Sun - rise,_____ Sun - set, Swift - ly_____ fly the

years;_____ One sea - son fol - low - ing an -

oth - er, Lad - en with hap - pi - ness and

tears._____

tears._____

rit.

From **"Fiddler On The Roof"** (1964)

If I Were A Rich Man

Lyrics by Sheldon Harnick
Music by Jerry Bock

man. *8va*

Would-n't have to work hard, Dai-dle, dee-dle, dai-dle,

dig-guh, dig-guh, dee-dle, dai-dle, dum. If I were a

bid-dy, bid-dy rich, dig-guh, dig-guh, dee-dle dai-dle man. I'd build a

big tall house with rooms by the doz-en, Right in the mid-dle of the town; A

Last time to Coda

Quasi rubato

rall.

Squawk-ing just as nois - i - ly as they can. And each loud

(imitate sounds)

quack and cluck and gob-ble and honk Will land like a trum-pet on the ear; As

D S. al Coda

if to say here lives a wealth-y man._____ *(Sigh)*

rall.

Coda

Tacet   Quasi rubato

man. I see my wife, my Gold - e, look-ing like a rich man's

Dai—dle, dee—dle, dai—dle dig-guh, dig-guh, dee—dle, dai—dle, dum.

Lord, who made the li—on and the lamb, You de—creed I should be what I am;

Would it spoil some vast e—ter—nal plan, If I were a wealth—y

man?

From **"On A Clear Day You Can See Forever"** (1965)

On A Clear Day (You Can See Forever)

Lyrics by Alan Jay Lerner
Music by Burton Lane

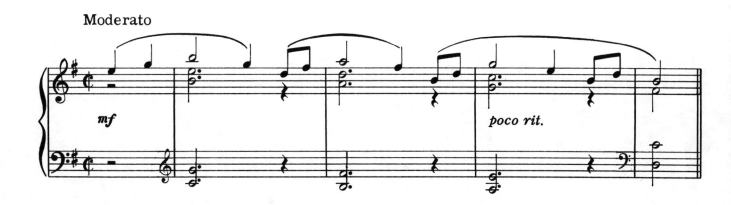

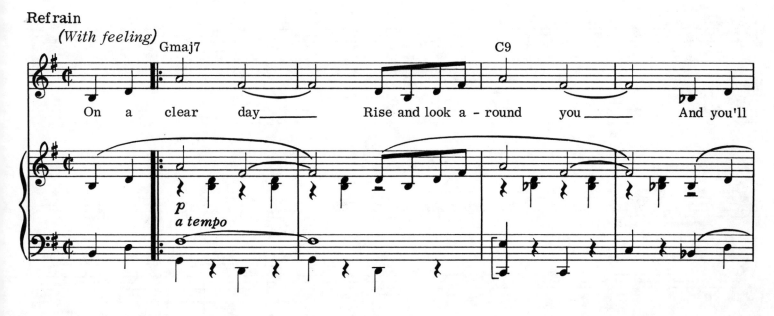

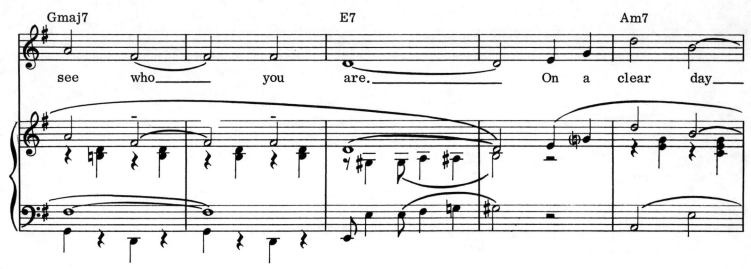

From **"Man Of La Mancha"** (1965)

The Impossible Dream

Lyrics by Joe Darion
Music by Mitch Leigh

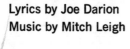

Tempo di Bolero

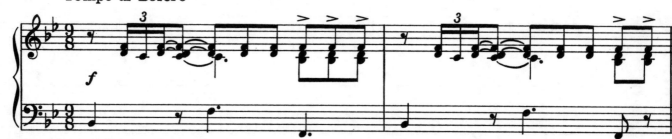

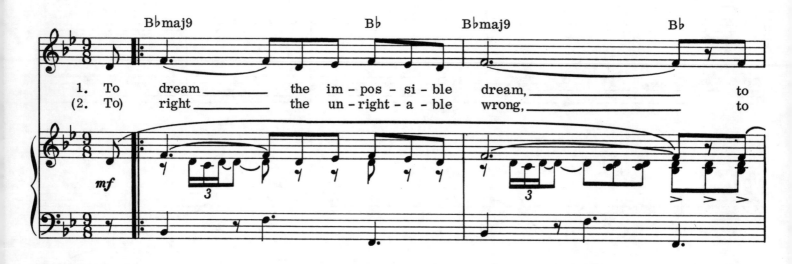

1. To dream the im-pos-si-ble dream, to
(2. To) right the un-right-a-ble wrong, to

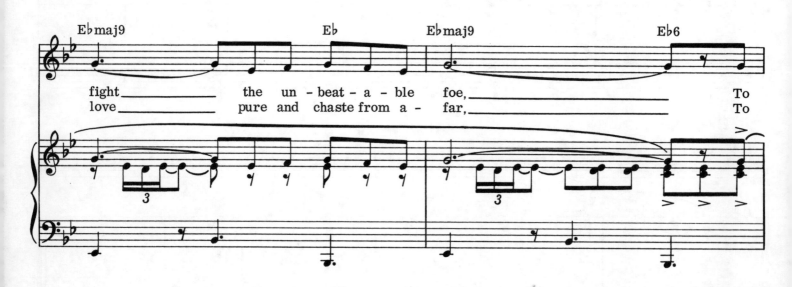

fight the un-beat-a-ble foe, To
love pure and chaste from a-far, To

rest,　　　　　　　And the world＿＿＿＿ will be bet-ter for

this;＿＿＿＿＿＿＿＿＿ That one man,＿＿＿＿＿ scorned and cov-ered with

scars,＿＿＿＿ Still＿ strove＿＿ with his last ounce of cour-age,＿＿＿＿＿ To

reach＿＿ the un-reach-a-ble stars.＿＿＿＿＿＿＿＿＿

From **"Cabaret"** (1966)

Cabaret

Lyrics by Fred Ebb
Music by John Kander

From **"Mame"** (1966)

Mame

Music & Lyrics by Jerry Herman

With a lilt

Chorus

1. You coax the blues right out of the horn, Mame,—
2. You've brought the cake walk back in-to style, Mame,—

You charm the husk right off of the corn, Mame,—
You make the weep-in' wil-low tree smile, Mame,—

From **"The Roar Of The Greasepaint—The Smell Of The Crowd"** (1967)

Who Can I Turn To (When Nobody Needs Me)

Music & Lyrics by Leslie Bricusse and Anthony Newley

Slowly, with expression

Who can I turn to ____ when no-bod-y needs me? ____ My

heart wants to know and so I must go where des-ti-ny leads me. ____ With

293

From **"Golden Rainbow"** (1968)

For Once In Your Life

Music & Lyrics by Walter Marks

From **"Zorba"** (1968)

Life Is

Lyrics by Fred Ebb
Music by John Kander

Moderato

Guitar:

Piano

(Play Bass notes 2nd time)

298

From **"Promises, Promises"** (1968)

I'll Never Fall In Love Again

Lyrics by Hal David
Music by Burt Bacharach

Rhythmically

What do you get when you fall in love,___ A {girl guy} with a pin to burst___

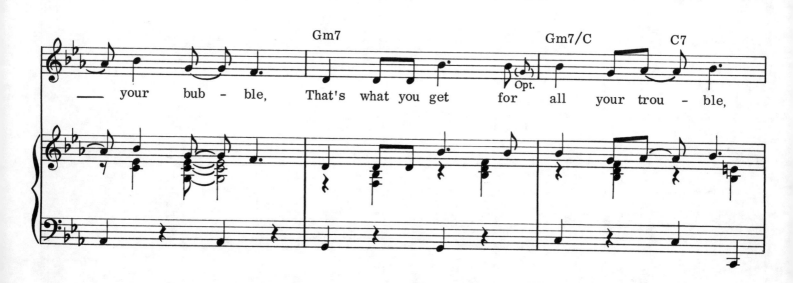

___ your bub - ble, That's what you get for all your trou - ble,

From **"Promises, Promises"** (1968)

Promises, Promises

Lyrics by Hal David
Music by Burt Bacharach

With fire

Prom-is-es, prom-is-es, I'm all through with prom-is-es, prom-is-es now! I don't know
Prom-is-es, prom-is-es, this is where those prom-is-es, prom-is-es end! I won't pre-

how   I got the   nerve_____ to walk   out._____ If I
tend   that what was   wrong_____ can be   right._____ Ev-'ry

From **"Godspell"** (1971)

Day By Day

Music & Lyrics by Stephen Schwartz

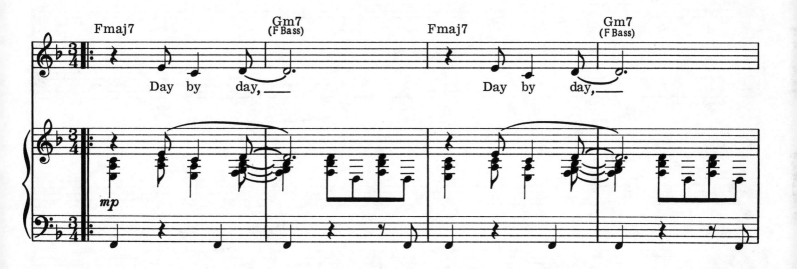

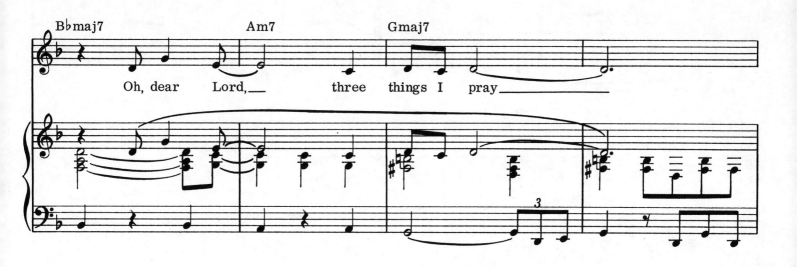

From "**Jesus Christ, Superstar**" (1971)

I Don't Know How To Love Him

Lyrics by Tim Rice
Music by Andrew Lloyd Webber

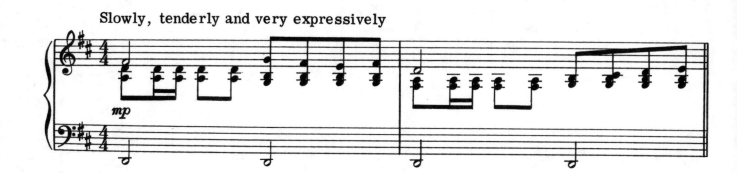

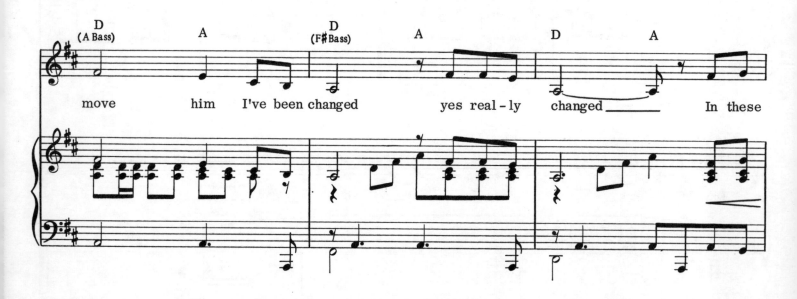

ver - y man - y ways He's just one more

Should I bring him down___ should I scream and shout___ Should I speak of love___

___ let my feel-ings out?___ I nev-er thought I'd come to this___ what's it all a-

bout?_____ Don't you think it's rath-er
Yet if he said he

CAMELOT — Playbill Cover

CAMELOT

BYE BYE BIRDIE

THE FANTASTICKS

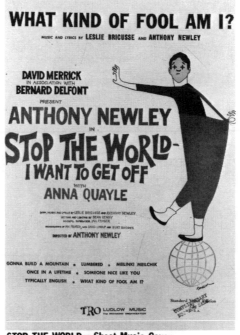

STOP THE WORLD — Sheet Music Cover

FUNNY GIRL — Playbill Cover

FIDDLER ON THE ROOF — Playbill Cover

MARQUEE — The Broadway Theatre

ON A CLEAR DAY YOU CAN SEE FOREVER

316

CLEAR DAY YOU CAN SEE FOREVER

MAN OF LA MANCHA — Sheet Music Cover

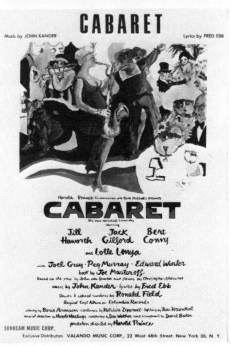

CABARET — Sheet Music Cover

— Playbill Cover

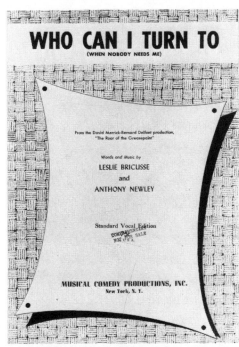

THE ROAR OF THE GREASEPAINT — Sheet Music Cover

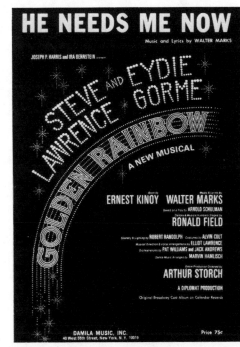

GOLDEN RAINBOW — Sheet Music Cover

A — Sheet Music Cover

PROMISES, PROMISES — Sheet Music Cover

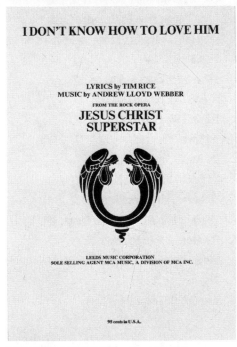

JESUS CHRIST, SUPERSTAR — Sheet Music Cover

Index of Songs

dex of Composers and Lyricists

Alan Jay Lerner is regarded as one of the theatre's most creative and brilliant artists. He has scored personal triumphs as a playwright, lyricist, screenwriter, essayist and producer. Two of his scripts share the distinction of being the only original screenplays for musicals to win Academy Awards. They are the memorable GIGI and AN AMERICAN IN PARIS.

Lerner attended Columbia Grammar School, New York; the Bedales School, Hampshire, England; the Choate School and Harvard University.

Broadway Musical Plays: WHAT'S UP, 1943; THE DAY BEFORE SPRING, 1945; BRIGADOON, 1947; PAINT YOUR WAGON, 1951; MY FAIR LADY, 1956; CAMELOT, 1960, above with Frederick Loewe. LOVE LIFE, 1948 with Kurt Weill; ON A CLEAR DAY YOU CAN SEE FOREVER, 1965 with Burton Lane; COCO, 1969 with Andre Previn.

Screen Plays: ROYAL WEDDING, 1951; AN AMERICAN IN PARIS, 1951; BRIGADOON, 1954; GIGI, 1958; MY FAIR LADY, 1964; CAMELOT, 1968; PAINT YOUR WAGON, 1969 (Also served as producer); ON A CLEAR DAY YOU CAN SEE FOREVER, 1970.

Academy Awards: 1951 Best Screen Play, AN AMERICAN IN PARIS; 1958 Best Screen Play, GIGI; 1958 Best Song, "Gigi".

Screenwriters Guild Award: 1951, AN AMERICAN IN PARIS; 1958, GIGI.
New York Drama Critics Circle Award: 1947, BRIGADOON; 1956, MY FAIR LADY.
Donaldson Award: 1956, MY FAIR LADY.
Antoinette Perry Award: 1956, MY FAIR LADY.
Grammy Award: 1966, ON A CLEAR DAY YOU CAN SEE FOREVER.
Christopher Award: 1954, BRIGADOON (Screen).

Elected to the Songwriters Hall of Fame in 1971. Serves on the Board of Governors of the National Hospital for Speech Disorders and the New York Osteopathic Hospital; President of the Dramatists Guild of America 1958 to 1963.

Jule Styne, one of Broadway and Hollywood's most talented composers, was born in London, England. He began studying music in Chicago at eight; appeared as piano soloist with the Chicago Symphony Orchestra at nine; studied piano, harmony, composition, and theory at Chicago College of Music.

Styne organized his own popular orchestra in Chicago, 1931, playing hotels and night clubs. He commenced working in motion picture studios in 1940 and has composed and produced for the theatre since 1947. He's composed over 30 motion picture scores, motion picture title songs, ballet scores, and New York stage production scores. Jule Styne has been oft-nominated for Hollywood's highest accolade, the Oscar, and received it for his song "Three Coins In The Fountain."

Songs:
ALL I NEED IS THE GIRL; AS LONG AS THERE'S MUSIC; BELLS ARE RINGING; BYE BYE BABY; CAN'T YOU JUST SEE YOURSELF; THE CHARM OF YOU; CHRISTMAS WALTZ; COMES ONCE IN A LIFETIME; CONCHITA MARQUITA LOPEZ; DANCE ONLY WITH ME; DIAMONDS ARE A GIRL'S BEST FRIEND; DON'T RAIN ON MY PARADE; EV'RY STREET'S A BOULEVARD IN OLD NEW YORK; EVERYTHING'S COMING UP ROSES; FADE OUT–FADE IN; FIVE MINUTES MORE; GIVE A LITTLE, GET A LITTLE; GUESS I'LL HANG MY TEARS OUT TO DRY; HOW DO YOU SPEAK TO AN ANGEL; I DON'T WANT TO WALK WITHOUT YOU; I FALL IN LOVE TOO EASILY; I FEEL LIKE I'M GONNA LIVE FOREVER; I'LL WALK ALONE; I MET A GIRL; I'M JUST TAKING MY TIME; I SAID NO; I STILL GET JEALOUS; IT'S BEEN A LONG, LONG TIME; IT'S MAGIC; IT'S THE SAME OLD DREAM; IT'S YOU OR NO ONE; I'VE HEARD THAT SONG BEFORE; JOHNNY FREEDOM; JUST A KISS APART; JUST IN TIME; LET IT SNOW, LET IT SNOW, LET IT SNOW; LET ME ENTERTAIN YOU; LITTLE GIRL FROM LITTLE ROCK; LONG BEFORE I KNEW YOU; MAKE SOMEONE HAPPY; NEVER NEVER LAND; ON A SUNDAY BY THE SEA; PAPA, WON'T YOU DANCE WITH ME; THE PARTY'S OVER; PEOPLE; PUT 'EM IN A BOX; RIDE ON A RAINBOW; SATURDAY NIGHT IS THE LONELIEST NIGHT IN THE WEEK; SAY, DARLING; SMALL WORLD; SOME PEOPLE; STAY WITH THE HAPPY PEOPLE; SUNDAY; THAT'S WHAT I LIKE; THERE GOES THAT SONG AGAIN; THINGS WE DID LAST SUMMER; THREE COINS IN THE FOUNTAIN; TIME AFTER TIME; TOGETHER WHEREVER WE GO; VICTORY POLKA; WHO ARE YOU NOW; YOU ARE WOMAN, I AM MAN; YOU LOVE ME; YOU MUSTN'T BE DISCOURAGED; YOU'RE MY GIRL.